Pleasures of the Game

Pleasures of the Game

Austin Allen

WAYWISER

First published in 2016 by

THE WAYWISER PRESS

Christmas Cottage, Church Enstone, Chipping Norton, Oxfordshire, OX7 4NN, UK
P.O. Box 6205, Baltimore, MD 21206, USA
http://waywiser-press.com

Editor-in-Chief
Philip Hoy

Senior American Editor
Joseph Harrison

Associate Editors
Eric McHenry | Dora Malech | V. Penelope Pelizzon | Clive Watkins
Greg Williamson | Matthew Yorke

9 7 5 3 1 2 4 6 8

A CIP catalogue record for this book is available from the British Library

ISBN 978-1-904130-82-6

Printed and bound by
T. J. International Ltd., Padstow, Cornwall, PL28 8RW

To my family and friends

ACKNOWLEDGMENTS

I am grateful to the following publications, in which some of these poems first appeared:

"Apollo," "Self-Portrait (The Desperate Man)," and "Sure" first appeared in *Prelude*.

"The Bargaining Bed" first appeared in *Linebreak*.

"The Constant Moons" and "For Halloween" first appeared in *Measure*.

"The Charm" first appeared in *The Missouri Review*.

"The House on St. Paul Street" first appeared in *Southwest Review*.

"Maris" first appeared in *Iron Horse Literary Review.*

"Ode to the Hartford Whalers" first appeared in *The Nervous Breakdown*.

"The Order of Her Room" first appeared in *River Styx*.

"Tamám Shud; or, Secrets in the Sand" first appeared in *The Yale Review*.

"Tower Scheherazade" and "Where He Is" first appeared in *32 Poems*.

"The Umpire" first appeared in *The Hopkins Review*.

"Valentine Variations" first appeared in *The New Guard*.

The verses that appear on the title page of each section are taken from Edward FitzGerald's translation of *The Rubáiyát of Omar Khayyám*. Sections I and III quote the 1859 edition; sections II and IV quote the 1889 edition.

Many thanks to Eavan Boland for her generous foreword to the book, and to Philip Hoy and V. Penelope Pelizzon of The Waywiser Press for their help with editing and design.

Special thanks to Mary Jo Salter and the faculty of the Johns Hopkins Writing Seminars, and to the many friends without whose advice, encouragement, and support this book would not have been possible.

Contents

Contents

Foreword by Eavan Boland

"I greatly enjoyed the highly formal patterns of those lyrics, as well, of course, as their wit and charm. In fact, the wit and charm seemed to have a lot to do with the formal patterns."

The words here belong to Anthony Hecht, the master poet for which this prize is named. They were part of an interview he gave to J. D. McClatchy in the *Paris Review* in 1988. Hecht's own poems – powerful, moving, and occasionally desolate – remain a standard of the appropriate relation between meaning and measure. Few poets in their time understood that relation so well. Few poets were able to show that form, as well as evincing wit and charm, could also deepen and darken the material it shaped.

His words, of course, couldn't include this year's winner of the Hecht prize and author of this book, Austin Allen. Nevertheless they have a very real application to the poems here. The first section, for instance, of this wonderfully assured, convincing work is called *The Games We Made*. It makes broad, musical brushstrokes across a variety of sports and endeavors. The Hartford Whalers. Roger Maris. A juggler so inexpert he wins the heart of a girl. The poet at thirteen as an umpire.

But look closely. The "highly formal patterns" in this section – Hecht's phrase again – suggest players betrayed by their games rather than made masters of them. The deft language in the second line of this couplet, for instance, gestures towards disguise, deception.

> I was the justice parents had to ask:
> the kid behind the kid behind the mask.

And there is more to come. Music, Syntax. Ambiguity. These old lyric mainstays are all on show. Each section of *Pleasures of the Game*, and there are four in all, is tagged with a quatrain from Edward FitzGerald's mid-nineteenth century translation, *The Rubáiyát of Omar Khayyám*: that thrilling power grab of Persian music on behalf of Victorian melancholy.

Each of the four sections in this book patterns its title on a phrase from the *Rubáiyát*. But more than phrases steal in. In his translation, FitzGerald played along with the shadows of determinism. In a wonderful short poem called "The Floating Café" Austin Allen does something of the same, bringing that dusk right into the contemporary moment.

> White walls, white tablecloth. We wedge in, order
> one glass noodle and one glass of water.
> (No other dish is mentioned on the menu.)
> A tray appears. Our lips from either end
> of the one tautening transparent strand
> converge with all the speed of Zen or Zeno.
> We're nearly halfway to the halfway mark.
> The walls and tablecloth are nearly dark.

The contemporary matters here. There is a striking intersection in *Pleasures of the Game* between iamb and rhyme and the modern landscape they flash over like summer lightning. This is important in terms of the conversation about form and poetry which certainly exists today, but all too often stalls. There is nothing nostalgic in the formal disposition of these poems. They are exhilarated by their moment, engaged by the paradoxes, ready for the experience.

If there is one poem that seems to embody all this more than any other it is "The Closing Doors" from the third section, *The Moon Who Knows*. In this marvelous micro-symphony of nods, winks, suggestions, inferences and sonnet-like concision a perfect snapshot of dailyness emerges. Here is everyone's experience of exits and exasperations. But here the experience happens in a world of dynamic ironies where literal movement collides with social reality. The lighted subway stairs to the train guides you to "rising fares". The line "You make your exit when the right time comes" is repeated just in case we miss how circular and self-deceiving our apparent progress is.

Goateed musicians with guitar and drums
play you offstage, and underneath the stage.
You make your exit when the right time comes.
You hear the night train in the cellarage
bellow and start to screech; you fly down stairs
that blaze a yellowish glow as arrows marked
on crossbeams guide you toward the rising fares.
You board. You feel as if you've disembarked.
Underground preachers thundering with rage
revise the theme; the undercarriage wails
its three-note song (the tune the audience hums
leaving the theater) as it sparks the rails,
and down the aisle a new musician strums.
You make your exit when the right time comes.

The speaker of "The Closing Doors" is the speaker of this book.
And like all the best speakers in poetry is a mix of music and con-
tradiction. On the one hand a wry, engaged and often resigned
announcer as far as the themes go. But on the other an exuber-
ant and activist maker of forms, urging us to look away from the
dark towards the light. And this, I have no doubt, is the speaker
the reader will follow willingly through this charmed adventure in
measure and meaning.

I.

The Games We Made

But leave the Wise to wrangle, and with me
The Quarrel of the Universe let be:
And, in some corner of the Hubbub couch'd,
Make Game of that which makes as much of Thee.

The Charm

Onyx locket.
Carven and dark, it
gleams from Bronx to tip.
Is found
each night, and stolen.
Burns
the same quick hole in
each thief's pocket,
gives each the slip.
Is washed clean underground
by that black market
out of which it came.
Returns
bearing your name.

Elementary

Here in the yard the game is underway:
a blend of soccer, tag, and Double Dutch,
co-ed and school-wide, no choice but to play,
no bench, no clock, no referee as such.
Winners get lunch. Losers hand over lunches.
The scene, as usual, is a free-for-all:
cheaters inflate their scores, bullies throw punches,
brats try to play the boss and hog the ball;
and one small clique, escaping all defeats,
quickly and sullenly, with black eyes, eats.

The next day everybody's had enough.
Huddling, the older kids make up a rule:
lunches for everyone—the weak, the tough,
the smart and dumb, unpopular and cool—
divvied up fairly, not as a reward
but "just as *lunch*." The players quit the game,
share, and sit still. Sit still. One boy grows bored
within five minutes, grabs a rock, takes aim—
and when the all-out, blood-soaked brawling ends
a half hour later, chows down with his friends.

If some whiz kid could figure out a balance—
guaranteed lunches with dessert as prize?
new ways of scoring to reward more talents?—
if grown-ups ever came to supervise;
if cliques were banished; if the kids weren't us
and we weren't always It, could skip a turn,
patch up our cuts, be rescued by a bus
or bell, file quietly inside and learn…
learn what? The game's back on. Our ears are ringing.
The swarms are clashing and the ropes are swinging.

The House on St. Paul Street

None of the bulbs could ever find the wattage
to really *light* the place, and half the switches
flipped the wrong way, and the wallpaper downstairs,
in the first two rooms, was a discolored cream
printed with pink buds, white buds, and green vines
in two different designs.
In the first-floor bathroom, the same basic scheme,
but with testicular-looking yellow pears.
Three floors, two fireplaces. A sort of cottage,
a sort of dorm. An embarrassment of riches.

Always six tenants, mostly students, always
rotating through (I moved, moved back again),
earning their stipends with pipette or pen,
falling in love or nodding in the hallways.
One whistled showtunes. One drove out the mice.
One cooked with lemon and asparagus spears.
(I lived on pub food, sandwiches, and rice.)
One called the cops in sudden fits of dread
about suspicious handprints on her bed,
or switches flipped the wrong way, or a heist...
What had been stolen? *Something*; she couldn't say.
The cops announced their suspect: "Poltergeist."
Four girlfriends in my room in those three years,
and one, who'd felt the Trade Towers falling, swore
she sensed a constant tremor in my floor.
I touched it: she was right.

And then the owner sold the place. I lay
stiff in a bedroll on that final night,
shivering. I'd told the owner I would leave
by midnight, come back midday to retrieve
a few stray items, so I woke to screaming:
"You are taking advantage, you are taking advantage!"
I grabbed my things and moved right down the block,

turned my new key, which snapped off in the lock
and sliced my hand, ran off and bought a bandage,
and landed in the old pub, still half-dreaming.

Ode to the Hartford Whalers

1979–97, Hartford, CT ("Insurance City")

I

I sing for the Hartford Whalers:
I mourn for a hockey team
that never, like Ahab's sailors,
dreamed the implausible dream,
or went down as hopeless flailers,
failing in the extreme.
They skated around their rink
and couldn't exactly sink.

II

In homeroom at age eight,
I studied, with fascination,
facts about my home state.
I worried: our population,
with its glacially slow growth rate,
was the tiniest in the nation
ever to try to support
a team in a big-league sport.

But there, in a vision of green,
they were and seemed to belong—
Shanahan, Burke, Dineen
(I number them all in my song)—
till, as I neared thirteen,
the facts proved all of them wrong.
The team would keep playing, but
not in Connecticut.

III

My own youth hockey days
had ended two years prior.
I'd set no ice ablaze

as a "Northern Connecticut Flyer";
nor, in my first growth phase,
had I shot all that much higher.
Still I stood tall and roared
whenever my Whalers scored…

> *The victory jingle, "Brass Bonanza,"*
> *fills the stadium, gives the fans a*
> *thrill. To this extravaganza*
> *I devote a special stanza.*

Suddenly hockey hurt:
the Whalers bowed, withdrew;
sports, in a final spurt,
outgrew me. Shortly I grew
out of my Whalers shirt,
my state—my family, too
(the fabric had started shrinking
and our population sinking).

IV

These days I live down south,
but I'm getting a chill again—
the draft I felt in youth,
joining the league of men.
Though all the teeth in my mouth
are accounted for, now as then,
in dreams they are missing, falling.
My team is my family, brawling.

And Hartford runs a correction
in small print in the *Courant*'s
editorial section:
"There's no such thing as insurance.
We lied for your protection.

Innocence builds endurance.
But lost is lost is lost:
now wake up and eat the cost."

Connecticut seems to remain.
My family has mostly gone.
I squint from a homebound train
at the capitol's snowbound lawn,
count each quaint weathervane,
assess what the weather's done…
But the place disclaims all claims.
I've stopped watching hockey games:

how can a grown man root
when the home team may just duck
out of its stadium, scoot
out of reach like a puck—
and home is no absolute,
either? With any luck,
love learns to improvise
on thin blades, on thin ice.

V

The town once threw a parade
when the Whalers survived the first
round of the playoffs. They played
decently—not their worst—
then lost as soon as they'd made
the point that they weren't cursed.
This happened when I was one;
then the glory days were done.

But what is athletic grace?
And who are sports' true heroes?
I watch a Zamboni trace

its Zen, concentric zeroes
on empty mental space.
Within that zone of clear O's,
one small black speck will go on
eluding me like a koan.

I sing for the team I loved
in a key that is cheerfully minor.
I mourn for the year they moved,
left my state with a shiner
(though the blow was politely gloved),
and settled in Carolina,
a market not quite as small.
The next year, they won it all.

The Umpire

What else could I get paid for at thirteen?
Ten bucks per A-League game in cold hard cash
to pad my wilted, rubber-banded stash—
plus, in the dusk at the concessions shed,
free food. The hotdogs hissed and spat. The green
soda fizz brimmed. The job went to my head.

I crouched. I screamed. I felt extremely grown-up.
Things hurtled at me and I made a choice
in my least terrified and squeaking voice.
I called it as I saw it. If I missed it
and someone called me on it, I insisted;
the training said you weren't supposed to own up.
I was the justice parents had to ask:
the kid behind the kid behind the mask,
wearing, behind my own, half-inch-thick lenses.
(I wanted more to signal than disguise
the newfound qualifications of my eyes.
Playing last year, I'd hardly seen the fences.)

Things smashed and ricocheted and soared and plopped.
My lenses fogged with sweat; I kept my cool.
Kids ran in shrieking circles; I backstopped
the chaos with my firm and book-based rule.
I fucked up nightly. Coaches weren't above
charging the plate and hurling anguished rage
at a kid not much more than their kids' age,
mouths twisting, golf tans reddening at their collars.
One called me "bitch." He did it out of love.
I took it for a hotdog and ten dollars.

In Mudville

Oh, somewhere in the alleys they've begun another game,
And the crowd still finds it thrilling, but the rules aren't quite the
    same,
And the layoffs at the gasworks have the watchmen carrying knives,
And the mayor wakes in dreams before a council of ex-wives.

Coyotes sniff the windowsills; the downtown streetlamps flicker;
The grown-ups look so solemn, all their teenage children snicker;
The men have special difficulty speaking to their fathers.
Mighty Casey finds it hardest. Nowadays he hardly bothers.

The music of the catcher's mitt, the fatal snap behind you,
Becomes a tune you learn by heart (though not on purpose, mind
    you)—
Repetition dulls the memory to an almost-pleasant thud;
Certain things must be expected in a town named after mud.

The wind-whipped foul poles whistle and the stand of bleachers
    creaks;
The chain-link fence is rusted stiff; the water fountain leaks;
The runoff floods the dugout till it rots the pinewood bench,
And the field is blooming, blooming, with the sweetness of the
    stench.

Maris*

* Roger Maris, American baseball player, famous for breaking Babe Ruth's single-season record of 60 home runs in 1961. Because Maris had a longer season than Ruth in which to accumulate his total, his feat generated fierce controversy, and one sportswriter suggested that an asterisk accompany his name in the record books. The commissioner of baseball agreed, but the mark was never added.

Asterisk, dark kiss, sign you were born under,
little appendix twinging in your gut,
making its clever point, its "Well yes but…"
Has someone carved it on your grave, I wonder?

It multiplies, becomes a flurry of flakes,
hardens to hail and pelts you as you run,
head lowered, one blast shy of sixty-one.
Litters its thistles, drives spikes through your spikes.

*

Babe Ruth ate the past. Which would have been
the present, back then. That huge son of a bitch
gobbled and guzzled, smoked and sinned so much,
what's left for you? The wine is drained, the women

know the score. Father of modern sport
and giant baby, hopeless little shit
sent to reform school, where he learned to hit,
and grin, and trot around the bases toward—

*

Rip the game stitch from stitch, green blade from blade.
Spill all the ball's yarn brains, the whole white mile
spooled to the core. You're starting to taste bile—
retch and spit up your black tobacco cud,

spit seeds, spit bubblegum, spit *it:* one spiked
windpipe obstruction like a Cracker Jack toy

lodged back there, somehow, since you were a boy...
You don't remember childhood much. You liked

baseball, liked summertime. Each place you lived
seemed colder than the last. Old tribal nations
under the fields, train platforms without stations.
Some years your parents quarreled and you moved.

You're not star-crossed; you don't believe in streaks;
statistically, things happen. Still, the team's
away games always give you hard-luck dreams:
Ruth's twenties roar, the cagefaced umpire blocks

your way, you can't reach—even to start from—home—
somehow the fix is in—each word you shout
at those fat folded arms is asterisked out...
The grass mends. The crowd goes tame. The seams resume.

*

Although it comes late, you hit that final blast.
The asterisk needs an asterisk of its own.
Above your Little League diamond, diamonds shone
unqualified....The record for time past

is broken, is broken. The child defeats the father,
memorabilia gathers on the shelf,
but time had more time to surpass itself,
so I'm not buying any of it, either.

Parabolic

The juggler was so adept
at making each fumbled ball
look like a part of the act—
each firm thud on the floor
a sacrifice toward a cause—
that he fumbled more and more,
till fumbling became, in fact,
his reason for juggling at all;
and at last, to ravished applause,
he fell on his knees and wept.

The girl he'd meant to impress
with the first set of balls he'd bought
came backstage to confess:
recently she had caught
every one of his shows.
Tonight she'd thrown him a rose...
As if to complete the arc
of their exact intent,
they caught a taxi and went
fumbling into the dark.

Transhumanism

"O brave new world..."

You can't get too much nakeder
than her,

or too much less
sober, and still play decent chess,

but if she puts more wine back,
she just might push that line back.

Over the pieces' heads I wink and smile.
We've been together a while

now, and evolved a certain sense of humor.
Nothing else lasts. You've heard that rumor,

or news—some science wizard trying to conjure
custom-made people: smarter, stronger,

sexier, less susceptible to cold,
or was it death? Well, such is getting old:

soon as you crawl ashore, adapt your tools,
the species changes rules.

We still play on the beach sometimes, my lover
and I. Stars fizz; the tide pours over and over.

I think our endgame might just be
the sea:

our books, games, selves
returning to its shelves—

jokes, too, which sink like rocks; a few unsolved
riddles, like quartz chips; all the rest dissolved

(not drowned). Our bodies finally fit enough,
we'll lose our shape—let go, like drunken love—

strip off the last taboo
and step into deep blue

as sea life jockeys to investigate...
She winks back, hits the clock. Two moves to mate.

II.

For Some We Loved

*For some we loved, the loveliest and the best
That from his Vintage rolling Time hath prest,
Have drunk their Cup a Round or two before,
And one by one crept silently to rest.*

Valentine Variations

I

Roses are red,
Violets are blue.
Spring has decided
To try someone new.

II

Violence is red,
Neurosis is blue.
The light in this bar
Has a purplish hue.

Frozen with dread,
Spineless straight through,
I drain half a wine bottle,
Plotting my coup.

Moses's Red
Dividing in two:
The crowd drains around her;
I stride up on cue.

Poses are shed.
Guileless blue
Eyes rise to meet me:
"No, I'll drink to *you*."

Cozy in bed…
Skylights imbue
Us with the reddening
Tinge of the view.

III

Rosé with bread.
Violins coo.
Candlelight melts
To a pool of white dew.

Goes to my head.
Wine hits me too.
Her eyes are diamonds,
My insides are goo.

Roses are red.
While this is true,
A man's got to do
What a man's got to do.

IV

"Oh yes," she says—
Violates a few
Ancient state laws
And a modern taboo—

Does all the things
I'd been begging her to,
Now that we're wed.
Somehow I'm blue.

V

Grossness is said,
Vileness spewed.
The door of the room
Of the night of the feud

Closes. A lead
Silence ensues.
A court case blows open.
We're both going to lose.

Noses are red,
Eyelids are too.
The case is straightforward.
My tie is askew.

VI

Roses are blue,
Violets are red.
Meanings are constructs.
The poem is dead.

Prose is unread,
Stylists are through.
Composers are next,
Says the *Paris Review*.

No, I misread—
Music went first.
I stare at my desk
And prepare for the worst.

Orchids are green!
Daisies are pink!
This wine's so delicious
I can't even think.

Cirrhosis ahead:
Bile will accrue.
Little by little
The bill will come due.

Roses are rose,
Violets are violet.
Love is clear prose;
Even dying won't style it.

Houses in rows—
Twilit, outspread.
The verdict is autumn.
I'm going to bed.

VII

Spring is in session,
The docket is full,
The heifer with bailiff eyes
Summons the bull,

Gold fuchsia indigo
Ochre vermilion
Are phlox poppies hyacinths
Mums by the billion,

Senses are evidence,
X equals Y,
And a couple in Paris
Decides with a sigh

That is subject to further
Judicial review
That roses are red
And that violets are blue.

Will They, Won't They

Will they or won't they? Should they? Should they not?
What if she slapped him just to keep things tense?
Which should they satisfy: themselves? The plot?
Those heartsick autocrats, the audience?

If he buys chocolates, which kind should he buy her?
Should she drop by the local dive he frequents?
Will joking friends or jealous foes conspire
To kill the slow chords of their daydream sequence?

How charming, really, is a charming klutz?
Will they age gracefully, if they must age?
When the projectile clocks him in the nuts,
why does his martyrdom resemble rage?

Would they be doing Earth a grave disservice
if they chose not to keep this spark alive?
Her hairbrush trembles—why is she so nervous?
Why does he keep returning to that dive?

Are they just patsies for their selfish genes
(their secret rivals)? Ages come and gone,
billions of lives milled like a hill of beans—
must we replace them? Really, what goes on

between the sheets? Before the sheepish edits?
How many chances can a species botch
before it sighs and fades to nameless credits?
Will you lean closer to me as we watch?

Sure

A fundamentally unserious man
asks you to dinner, laughing, "I insist."
Can you refuse? You can't be sure you can.

Although he isn't handsome, tall, or tan
(you could add other *isn't*s to the list),
this fundamentally unserious man

seems half sincere—and what's more tempting than
being with two minds at once? You can resist,
yes, but refuse? You can't be sure you can.

Who said love has to taste like powdered bran?
Why not permit your plot a little twist?
The fun, the generally unserious man

at least has no grand hopes, no ripening plan;
the one-track types, as long as they persist,
you can refuse. You can't be sure you can

this time…and afterwards, on your divan,
who knows? Once you've already sort of kissed
this fundamentally unserious man,
can you refuse? You can't be sure. (You can.)

For Halloween

Vodka blood punch, communion with the host
who is Paul Bunyan and already drunk,
two wolves, a wine-stained Roman and a ghost
whose tattered hem and silver-powdered breasts
and laughter seem to trail me all night, hovering—
I the nefarious, hairy Russian monk
still swallowing draughts of poison and recovering.

Petticoats! Tweeds and weaves! Baubles and bangles!
All clothes are pulled out of a dress-up trunk.
Why don't more parties end with all the guests
huddled by flashlight in their flesh and fur,
telling their stories with the rags torn off their chests?
That's what they seem to want. As I want her—
over the bed, moon low, ghost linen at her ankles.

Gossip

As Keats loved the nightingale
that blabbed on its backwoods perch,
as Chaucer loved a good tale
and Frost a solid birch,

as Rilke loved giving advice,
as Tennyson loved to grieve,
as Milton loved paradise
but lusted after Eve,

as Millay loved to throw
a man away once she'd caught him,
as Verlaine loved Rimbaud
so tenderly that he shot him,

as Dickinson with shy sadness
loved "Master," who dismissed her,
as Byron loved madness, badness,
danger, and his half-sister,

as Auden loved a blond boy
and some ironic God,
as Yeats loved Helen of Troy
(who was really an ex named Maud),

as Blake loved angels and Zoas,
as Marianne Moore loved fish,
pelicans, snails, jerboas,
and dragons; as Percy Bysshe

Shelley aspired to marry
the soul of humankind,
and said that our loves must vary
and hoped his wives wouldn't mind,

as Langston Hughes loved the blues,
as Ted Hughes trembled for Plath
at night; as Plath loved Hughes
at the height of her righteous wrath,

as Williams loved rebirth,
as Eliot loved dry bone,
as Wordsworth loved Wordsworth,
as Larkin loved being alone,

as Bishop doted on Lota
(and Lowell, but from a distance),
as Whitman loved every iota
of his painfully strange existence—

may the grass be the witness thereof!—
as Apollinaire loved a whore,
as Neruda loved pure love
and liked fucking even more,

as sonnets loved Thomas Wyatt,
John Donne, and Gwendolyn Brooks,
as a haiku loves quiet,
as quiet loves books,

as Homer loved the ocean
and Virgil the underworld gloom
and Dante his own devotion
and Shakespeare God knows whom—

I want to love you in words
that sing without spilling the goods,
like the empty gossip of birds
in the ignorant backwoods.

The Bargaining Bed

You joined me, last night, in the bargaining bed,
in the deep reasonableness of dreams,
and much of what could be said (it should be said)
was not, but midnight saw the major themes

touched on, at least—as family and friends meanwhile
slipped through the door, and sat by us, and peered
with excellent bedside manner and small smile,
then drifted out until the room had cleared—

and there were strange adjustments: head to foot
we lay, then back to back, then face to face.
Shifting and shifting. Till the stars were moot,
and a sense dawned of things proceeding apace.

The Floating Café

White walls, white tablecloth. We wedge in, order
one glass noodle and one glass of water.
(No other dish is mentioned on the menu.)
A tray appears. Our lips from either end
of the one tautening transparent strand
converge with all the speed of Zen or Zeno.
We're nearly halfway to the halfway mark.
The walls and tablecloth are nearly dark.

The Order of Her Room

Buddhism it was not.
Maybe it was, a bit.
Maybe the opposite,
which nonetheless contained
the part that she'd been taught,
and from which we abstained.

We didn't live in sin.
We didn't share the lease
or any special rites
except eating, most nights,
from a Vietnamese
or Thai food tin,

or the same cereal bowl
with separate spoons.
Maybe part Buddhism,
and on the whole
not bad. Half nudism
some afternoons—

her towels hung as drapes,
plain pink or striped,
screening us from the street,
rooftops and fire escapes.
In Sunday summer heat
we sat topless and typed.

Although it was her space,
I lingered in it more.
Days when I worked from home,
her home, I sat in place
and watched her go and come
bone-tired through the door.

My radiologist
in training, she would fall
asleep after her call
still wearing her white robe,
as I lay close and kissed
the flesh of one earlobe.

Unpierced and simple.
After her virtuous nap
she'd rise and wash,
reenter with panache
in a pink towel wimple
that dripped in her lap

as she sat down and tried
to work. With me beside
and just the towel on.
So I angled to play—
wanted, like some charged ray,
to be absorbed, indrawn,

and find…well, what?
What *is* the body's center?
Can it be reached or not?
How shall the seeker enter?
Quizzing her flesh and bone,
I hardly knew my own—

until I passed, somehow,
beyond the windowpane,
out to the fire escape
from which I peer back now.
Striped towel, undrape
the radiance of that scene…

We sit in our bare skin,
crossing our legs, and read,
and write. Our knees may touch
a little, but not much.
If we have any need
at all, we'll order in.

Calliope

Round and round,
round and round.
Who is the muse?
Whose muse is whose?

Soon as you've found
you're bound to lose.
Why choose to choose?
Round and round.

2

No pedestal:
that's what makes her so sweet,
you've told yourself. Already as tall
as she'll ever need to be: nine feet.
She'll kick away whatever's built beneath her—
and beneath you, so don't try that one, either.

She writes herself,
you know. No call
to serve on her behalf:
it's all under control.

She speaks feelingly of a man
she tried and failed to win.
Blond, with an athlete's strength.
One night with the lights still on,
she lay along him, along all his length,
almost, since he was nine foot one,
and tried to choose him, but it was no use.
Between them a seeming geometric line—
all his caresses tender but abstruse.

It's tough all around
and round and round…

3

Her smile a twitch.
A puckish pucker, intermittent.
Think of the way you'd suck a small, sweet mint.

Slight hitch or catch—
something about to hatch.

4

You are avid, you are pent.
You are gravid with intent.

You feel, even at rest,
the pressure on your chest

and between your thighs.
You lie flat, close your eyes,

clench fists and teeth and toes
till even your organs close—

but the song that you release
is a steamboat organ's wheeze.

The only dance it rouses
is a cartoon mouse's.

Or it's a fairground sound
that cycles round and round…

5

Two hundred thousand men
contending for a woman
all will lose
but one. Whose muse is whose?

The campfires flicker.
Grown men bicker
over a girl at a degree's remove
from the alleged love.
Who, for her part, can't choose,
perched on her battlement
above the fray. Who's no one's muse—
shrugs off entitlement,
refuses honors and recuses herself,
won't even watch the battle, loses herself
in a little puff of smoke, a little booze...

6

The vivisection of rejection
opens you lengthwise like a trout.
She weighs and studies every part,
knowing she's going to throw you out—
not for a freckle and not for a mole,
not for a presence and not for a lack,
she doesn't know why but it isn't your heart
and it isn't your brain and there isn't a soul;
you are being turned down whole.
Being sewn up and thrown right back—
the choice is final and so she throws,
and you catch a last smile and know she knows.

7

At last she inspires you to write
something that's very long.
Something is very wrong.

You are writing a letter.
There is pronoun confusion:
to what is "all of this" a vague allusion?
"I had had certain feelings"—is that right,
or is the present perfect better?
To insert, or not, a joke?
What sounds colloquial? What sounds baroque?

The letter is getting
longer, getting wronger.
You see where all of this is heading:
you've sent it before,
repented before,
said that it made you stronger.

So it did: your wrist
is hardly burning…
The letter is longhand and is turning
into a catalogue, an endless list.

8

"Two tragedies,"
someone lies:

"not getting what you want
and getting what you want."
You learn the world is terrible
or that you are terrible.
You know which is more bearable.

9

How does the muse
relate to Zeus?

They are one theme.
Her father, godly,
watching from his mountain,
making no descent.
Still dreadfully present.

In a dream
she feels him at her shoulder,
approving, disapproving. Oddly,
so do you. You're getting older.
To what, in fact, are you amounting?

You know, it isn't widely understood
how far he rose. He started out with nothing,
and she would do the same thing if she could—
already drives a plain car, wears plain clothing,

but keeps alternatives if needed.
(If there's a judgment to be heeded.)

10

Taste isn't always tact
but she has both. You've been refused
enough to know how masterful this was—
a triumph of plain style:
clear eyes, clear voice, clear heart,
and the slight hitch of her smile
only slightly amused.

You want to say, in fact,
this is her art,
is what she *does*—
but how do you know what she does?

That's just the point.
Who plays the muse to whom?
She writes herself. Who knows? She might anoint
herself each night, in the quiet of her room.

11

Round and round.
Whose muse is whose?
Pronouns shift
and shifts confuse—

*she*s become *you*s,
*you*s become *me*s
with fluid ease,
but you get the drift.

Trojans have burned,
Greeks have drowned.
What have we learned?
Plunk the keys,

play the jingle
and change the scene.
Don't sing a single
word you mean,

but warm to the love
of plain damn sound.
If it wants you enough,
you might come around.

III.

The Moon Who Knows

Ah, Moon of my Delight who know'st no wane,
The Moon of Heav'n is rising once again:
How oft hereafter rising shall she look
Through this same Garden after me—in vain!

Apollo

We have a problem.
Are we forgetting something?
The moon climbs,
and somehow we can't
quite seem to place the face.
And this happens sometimes.

We have a problem:
the moon falls
just out of reach, between the hills,
like one of the golf balls
from the old Apollo mission.
Did we leave something behind?

We seem to recall—there was a flag,
artificially stiffened
because there was no wind.
And a little plaque signed
by the president, Nixon.
In five o' clock shadow,
he lost the debate
to the younger fellow,
but now the harsher face is on the rise.

Are we forgetting something?
Did we leave someone behind?
One of the astronauts, the handsome fellow—
Apollo?
No, that was the name of the mission.
The name on the little plaque had to be Nixon.
And quarters, halves, bits of loose change
wink—sink between the cushions
of the distant hills.

Tower Scheherazade

Again the death-plot
has miscarried:
she's kept her head,
she isn't married—
not by her lights—
and on her cot
(which isn't his bed)
through hot, hushed nights,
she conjures, hour
by hour, from vapor,
a mind's-eye tower
of unbound paper:
one thousand stories
or just one, climbing
slow as the moon
of shifting glories,
looming immune
to quakes and fires;
a stock-still, sky-tall
shrine to timing,
which she'll let fall
when she desires...

The Closing Doors

Goateed musicians with guitar and drums
play you offstage, and underneath the stage.
You make your exit when the right time comes.
You hear the night train in the cellarage
bellow and start to screech; you fly down stairs
that blaze a yellowish glow as arrows marked
on crossbeams guide you toward the rising fares.
You board. You feel as if you've disembarked.
Underground preachers thundering with rage
restate the theme; the undercarriage wails
its three-note song (the tune the audience hums
leaving the theater) as it sparks the rails,
and down the aisle a new musician strums.
You make your exit when the right time comes.

The Guitar

(After Lorca)

The guitar
begins to cry again.
Dawn's cup
is smashed: it bleeds
a bright wine stain.
The guitar
begins to cry again.

It won't shut up.
It can't shut up.
Abacus
of the lugubrious,
methodical totter-
up of teardrop beads:
rain on the water,
snowflakes on a plain…

It wants what's far.
It cries,
wheedles and wails—
desert forever
parched for some
cool blossom,
targetless dart…
(Some poor bird's eyes
glaze over.)
Gone, guitar,
out of itself: your heart
still needled by five nails.

The Strawberry Blonde in the Mustard Field

for L.P.

Late Sixties. Fall.
A troupe of actors takes
a slow bus ride
through mellow countryside.

They're packed like clowns.
One leans out to admire
the scenery: dreamy farms
and folklore towns.

He sees her first.
She keeps a roadside stand—
*the strawberry blonde
in the mustard field,*

as, ever since,
he's called her in his head.
Who's *something else,*
hawking her jars and tins.

How many customers
could pass this way—
five, ten per day?
His karma beams at hers.

They barter small talk…
He takes home no more
than this one minor piece
of private lore.

The bus trails off
into a strawberry sun.
Kicks up what must
be mustard-colored dust.

Two summers later
on another tour,
the troupe will play
to an audience of four

during the first moon landing.
Somewhere she is standing
in her own ovation
at her stand.

Where He Is

When did more people weep for Johnny Carson:
during the last show or the emphysema's
follow-up act? Tonight, how many weep?
Tonight he owns the time slot of my sleep.
I dream the L.A. leisure suit; I dream his
prairie-boy charm as he invites the stars in—

really a pageant of my own lost friends
restored: and here's Johnny, and here they are,
as I sit hidden in the studio rafters.
Lavaliers catch and swell their separate laughters.
The host bends at his desk as at a bar
to ask how far the heart's career extends—

and in mid-sentence, starts to hack and cough
till the sound cuts out and the lights wink off.

Self-Portrait (The Desperate Man)

Gustave Courbet, c. 1845

Consider my face.
Is it handsomely desperate
or just desperately handsome?
Is each clutched hair in place?

Notice the crimson flush
upon each cheek.
Is that a fever's rose
or rouge, do you suppose?
If rouge, would my mystique
be heightened? Would you blush?

With whom do I share
this elegant despair?

Such arrogance
as I must have to boast,
"I am the most
arrogant man in France":

is it not also yours?
Who but yourself, indulging,
summons the force
that draws me in, distorts
my eyes, my ego bulging
toward the terror's source—

which (it could not be clearer)
is a mirror?

Portrait of the Brontës with the Artist Removed

1834. National Portrait Gallery, London.

Branwell Brontë has painted himself out.
His last faint trace floats in a ghostly column.
A spaceship's tractor beam. A ray of doubt.
His sisters stand with him, intact and solemn.

They stand with Branwell as he melts in air,
those three weird sisters with their sheer blue shawls
and their uncommonly intense red hair.
A beam shines down from heaven: something calls.

Branwell is gone. The painting isn't bad
save for the awkward fact of his removal.
He's gone to the pub. Gone into debt. Gone mad.
Charlotte smiles grimly, but with faint approval.

She knows in twenty years they'll all be dead.
The alien beam of light is tinted red.

The Constant Moons

Out of Uranus,
out of the clear blue sky,
inside the inmost ring,
during a certain phase,

lighting a cigarette
(the atmosphere somehow
seems to allow it),
Universe, to you

I speak. Words plucked
from the galaxy's whorled ear.
Out of Uranus. Presto:
out of strange, thin air.

> *Exit Titania, exit Oberon,*
> *exit Miranda, Ariel, and Umbriel.*

Universe, I place my faith
in you. Where else?
Out of a secret pocket
in the bureaucracy of stars,

a loophole in the fabric,
you will manage to pluck—
on my behalf—a moon.
You'll pull some strings.

I will seize the trailing locks
of opportunity's comet,
hightail away
astride a nebulous horse.

Exit Cordelia, Ophelia, and Bianca.
Exit Cressida, Desdemona, Juliet.
Exit Portia and Rosalind, pursued by Cupid.
Exit Belinda, Perdita, Puck, and Mab.

Some distant night,
on some Plutonian shore
by a nitrogenous river,
all the dead shall meet,

and smoke, and act
much as they did before.
Drinking their green caipirinhas
on a moraine slope.

Or their twins will,
or the twins of their twins.
Only a little different,
under a Charon moon.

Exit Francisco, exit Caliban,
exit Stephano, Trinculo, and Sycorax.
Exit tardy Margaret, hasty Prospero,
retrograde Setebos, distant Ferdinand.

Exeunt omnes.
Goodnight, moons.
Goodnight, you sinking gods
and dwindling men.

Into the curtsy
of gravity you dip,
sweet ladies. Goodnight.
Until we meet again.

My cigarette dwindles
in a nice slow burn.
Goodnight. You've all
been lovely. Until soon.

> *Silence a while, then a stirring within.*
> *Enter Titania rising in her turn.*

IV.

About the Secret

Would you that spangle of Existence spend
About the Secret—Quick about it, Friend!
A Hair perhaps divides the False and True—
And upon what, prithee, may life depend?

Tamám Shud; or, Secrets in the Sand

Australia's most famous cold case is the mystery of "Somerton Man," found dead on Somerton Beach, Adelaide, in 1948. Coroners could not identify the toxin that killed him, police could not prove or rule out foul play, and cryptographers could not solve the code that surfaced in connection with the case. The man's name and origins remain unknown.

"WRGOABABD / ~~MLIAO~~ / WTBIMPANETP /
MLIABOAIAQC / ITTMTSAMSTGAB"

I. *The Write-Up*

It's done. The tide is calm. The coast is clear
for miles around the man the dawn finds here,
back to a wall, feet pointing toward the sea.
The first inquiring fly crawls in his ear.

*   *   *

Items in his possession: used bus ticket,
unused rail ticket, matches, cigarette packet
(labeled a different brand than what's inside),
chewing gum, comb—and in a hidden pocket,

found four months afterward, a sort of note
torn from a book. The words the poet wrote
to close *The Rubáiyát*: a Persian phrase
ineptly typing fingers soon misquote,

for some newspaper write-up, as *Taman
Shud*. The word's *Tamám*. Errors will spawn
errors: the standard label for the case
becomes *Taman Shud* and the case goes on.

No solid leads. Some theories disproved,
but none confirmed. No name, no one he loved
or hated, no official cause of death.
No wallet. Labels on his clothes removed.

Tamám Shud; or, Secrets in the Sand

*   *   *

November thirtieth, 1948:
a man runs toward his train, which doesn't wait.
He checks his bag and takes a bus instead,
finds the address, knocks on the door—too late.

She's gone. He shivers, wanders toward the sand.
En route he marks the slim book in his hand
with her unlisted number and a code,
carries it past the glare of parked cars, and,

spying a rolled-down window, stops to throw it
onto the seat. Someone will find it, show it
to the police—not right away, of course…
The book's *The Rubáiyát*, but he's no poet.

The code—well, it's a sort of inside joke.
Down at the shore he strolls, a fortyish bloke,
hair graying. Buys a pasty. Hurls some stones.
Leans on the seawall and lights up a smoke.

The poison, mingling with the cigarette's
familiar poisons, fills his lungs. He lets
himself relax, experiencing—what?
A touch of dizziness, but no regrets.

No one he knows will genuinely grieve.
He carries, like a last trick up his sleeve,
the torn-out fragment of *The Rubáiyát*
in his fob pocket. He does not believe

in prayer—prays anyway, to all the gods.
A man in his profession plays the odds.
He's heard of Pascal's wager, bets on Yes,
but knows that No awaits him when he nods.

II. *The Agent*

No one can place him, so he's quickly cast
as national myth, a creature of this vast
unlikely island-country-continent
proud of its oddball fauna, outlaw past,

and shining harbors: Sydney, Melbourne, Perth.
For any misfit dreaming of rebirth
into a pleasant anonymity
or interested in falling off the earth,

Australia holds a certain fascination…
The bag the man left at the railway station
contains mislabeled clothes, some tools, a knife.
Theorists whisper *spy*—but for which nation?

The Cold War's underway. The town lies near
a missile test site, built the previous year.
When rumor has it that the world might end,
even the world's edge feels the thrill of fear.

Anyone, everyone might be a spy—
your pleasant-looking neighbors, you and I,
chain-smoking strangers who give up the ghost
at night, on lonely shores, and who knows why?

*   *   *

He has time to consider what he's done.
This, then—this beach, this wall at Somerton—
this was the plan? Will she be satisfied?
Down from the foothills in the straggling sun

a perfume drifts: astringent, eucalyptic.
And was it such a pleasure, being cryptic?

Everyone knows the world ends when you go
(that's why the old grow so apocalyptic)—

why not scream out at last? Why all the lying,
hedging, and hinting? Why the harebrained spying,
ciphering, scheming, right until the end?
And why this shadiest evasion, dying?

Couldn't they both have wound up like those saps
who draw elaborately misleading maps
around their buried hearts; dig moats, lay traps;
then fall precisely in each other's laps?

Maybe he ought to grab a stick and write
all of their secrets in the sand, for spite…
No. No regrets, no rage. He owes himself.
Besides, his arm's numb and there's not much light.

Slowly they vaporize: home country, name,
affairs, affiliations, motives, blame…
And if it's true about her infant son,
will *he* appreciate the hunt—the game?

*   *   *

….Or was it murder? Plot the stratagem—
dream up a theory till you're there with them
behind the brass rail of a seaside bar,
behind his eyes as they trail up her hem,

inside his head as it swells up with booze.
Argue about whose country's worse than whose;
feel your limbs start to ache—the walls, her words
close in: "The kind of war where both sides lose"—

then watch her go, this bombshell local nurse
turned mild-eyed agent of the universe
who pays the tab and leaves you sorting out
what's guile, what's innocence, and which is worse...

And when, at last, polite detectives ring
her number, call her in for questioning,
wheel out the body and peel back the sheet,
she stares, turns pale—and doesn't know a thing.

III. *My Life Is All But Over, And I Am Quite Content*

The plot spins outward...theories spawn and thrive
far longer than the dead man was alive.
The *Rubáiyát* she gave a soldier friend—
the one found on a corpse in '45,

the brother of a barrister—the trails
diverging, fading out—false tips, tall tales—
pins spreading like a pox across the map—
aircraft from Russia, trains from New South Wales—

how deep does this thing go? And as one delves,
will one find subterranean hives of elves,
long-vanished continents, the face of God,
but never solve this man? Is he ourselves?

Is this a station gate through which we pass
like tourists, separately and yet en masse—
a guise we're all someday assigned to wear,
like "wave" or "grain of sand" or "blade of grass"?

Will we restage his triumph: don the mask,
drop the prop cigarette, lie back and bask
in silence....Or was this his act alone?
Is it a kind of sabotage to ask?

Time warp, black hole—whatever trick he played,
whichever flaw he crawled through to evade
the whole regime—outwit the scheme of things—
should we withdraw and let him lounge in shade,

in sand, in mystery, cool grains of which
swirl through his final scene, invade and itch
the secret regions of the gathering crowd
that frowns, "Who *is* he—poor son of a bitch"?

IV. *World's End*

He never planned to stir up this much fuss.
He took a solitary trip by bus,
swallowed or smoked a toxin from a plant,
followed a route available to us.

The case goes on and will be laid to rest.
Nothing was ever proven or confessed,
yet there he lies, a few feet underfoot.
Reality goes nowhere and knows best

and, badgered long enough, stammers a clue.
"A hair perhaps divides the false and true"—
seize that hair! Tweeze it, freeze it in the lab,
demand it tell you on whose head it grew—

haul in the bones—probe with unflinching touch—
pluck something—one grain—from the hand's stiff clutch—
decrypt the grin. Snoop! Pry! Has any true
spy ever died because he knew too much?

*　　*　　*

The poison's slow. He tries to smile. *Tamám
Shud:* "It is done." At least he'll dodge the Bomb,

the worst of love…his stomach feels like hell
and all along the shore the earth breathes calm.

He knows, he knows—her son, her soldier friend,
her fiancé—that's why he had to send
so chaste and intimate a code. His life's
a scratched-out error, but this careful end

will be the one clear fact for which it vouches.
Against the wall at Somerton he slouches.
Across the continent fantastic beasts
tuck the most marvelous secrets in their pouches—

he knows—he senses, like a lifelong ranger,
some transformation in the land—some danger
lacing the wind…he opens his eyes wide
and greets the ocean like a total stranger.

A Note About the Author

Photograph: © Summer Greer

Austin Allen was born in Middletown, Connecticut, in 1984. He received an MFA in Poetry from Johns Hopkins University in 2012 and has worked as a book editor, teacher, and digital archivist. His poetry and essays have appeared widely in print and online. He has taught as a lecturer in creative writing at Johns Hopkins University and currently lives in Cincinnati, Ohio, where he studies and teaches at the University of Cincinnati.

Other Books from Waywiser

Other Books from Waywiser

Bradford Gray Telford, *Perfect Hurt*
Matthew Thorburn, *This Time Tomorrow*
Cody Walker, *Shuffle and Breakdown*
Cody Walker, *The Self-Styled No-Child*
Deborah Warren, *The Size of Happiness*
Clive Watkins, *Already the Flames*
Clive Watkins, *Jigsaw*
Richard Wilbur, *Anterooms*
Richard Wilbur, *Mayflies*
Richard Wilbur, *Collected Poems 1943-2004*
Norman Williams, *One Unblinking Eye*
Greg Williamson, *A Most Marvelous Piece of Luck*
Greg Williamson, *The Hole Story of Kirby the Sneak and Arlo the True*
Stephen Yenser, *Stone Fruit*

FICTION
Gregory Heath, *The Entire Animal*
Mary Elizabeth Pope, *Divining Venus*
K. M. Ross, *The Blinding Walk*
Gabriel Roth, *The Unknowns**
Matthew Yorke, *Chancing It*

ILLUSTRATED
Nicholas Garland, *I wish ...*
Eric McHenry and Nicholas Garland, *Mommy Daddy Evan Sage*
Greg Williamson, *The Hole Story of Kirby the Sneak and Arlo the True*

NON-FICTION
Neil Berry, *Articles of Faith: The Story of British Intellectual Journalism*
Mark Ford, *A Driftwood Altar: Essays and Reviews*
Richard Wollheim, *Germs: A Memoir of Childhood*

* Co-published with Picador